P9-DWD-657

Adding around the City

Rann Roberts

CAPSTONE PRESS
a capstone imprint

First hardcover edition published in 2011 by
Capstone Press
151 Good Counsel Drive, P.O. Box 669, Mankato, MN 56002
www.capstonepub.com

Published in cooperation with Teacher Created Materials. Teacher Created Materials
is a copyright owner of the content contained in this title.

Editorial Credits

Dona Herweck Rice, editor-in-chief; Lee Aucoin, creative director; Sara Johnson,
senior editor; Jamey Acosta, associate editor; Neri Garcia and Gene Bentdahl,
designers; Stephanie Reid, photo editor; Rachelle Cracchiolo, M.A. Ed., publisher;
Eric Manske, production specialist

Library of Congress Cataloging-in-Publication Data
Roberts, Rann.
   Adding around the city / by Rann Roberts.
      p. cm. —(Real world math)
   Includes index.
   ISBN 978-1-4296-6840-8 (library binding)
   1. Addition—Miscellanea—Juvenile literature. 2. Cities and towns—Miscellanea—
Juvenile literature. I. Title. II. Series.
   QA115.R63 2011
   513.2'11—dc22   2011001573

Image Credits

Dreamstime/Banol2007, 5; Gerald Bernard, 9
Getty Images/Giorgio Cosulich, 24 (back)
iStockphoto/Jyeshern Cheng, 4
Shutterstock/Albert Lozano, 25; Brasiliao, 17; Chris Jenner, 10; Christopher
      Dodge, 22–23; Clara, 26 (top); Drimi, 14 (top); EVRON, 16; Ilja Mašík, cover, 1;
      Jan Kranendonk, 7 (bottom); Merrill Dyck, 18–19; mikeledray, 11; Mirko, 14
      (bottom); Oksana Perkins, 20–21; Philip Lange, 7 (top), 8; Reinhold Foeger, 27;
      Sochigirl, 12–13; Svetlana Larina, 26 (bottom); Tom Mc Nemar, 24 (front)

Printed in the United States of America in Stevens Point, Wisconsin.
032011   006111WZF11

Table of Contents

Off We Go!

We were going to the city for spring break! I had some homework to do. I needed to keep track of all the ways I used **addition** on my trip.

First we drove to the airport. Next we flew on a plane. The airport was big! When we landed, a shuttle took us to the subway. That was 4 types of **transportation** already!

The subway is a commuter train. It goes below the ground. We bought our tickets. We used addition to figure out how much money the tickets cost.

Subway Ticket Prices

Day Ticket for Child	$1.00
Day Ticket for Adult	$2.00
Week Ticket for Child	$4.00
Week Ticket for Adult	$10.00

LET'S EXPLORE MATH

The family needed to buy 5 subway tickets. They thought they would use the subway all week. So they bought the week tickets. Look at the ticket costs. Then answer the questions.

a. An adult's ticket for 1 week costs $10. How much would 2 tickets cost?

b. A child's ticket for 1 week costs $4. How much would 3 tickets cost?

c. How much did the family pay for 2 adult week tickets and 3 child week tickets?

The subway took us right to our hotel.

We took an **escalator** to the street. I saw cars, taxis, and buses there. Some people walked or rode bikes.

There were 11 taxis parked on the street in front of the hotel. There were 12 taxis outside another hotel around the corner. I used addition. That made 23 taxis in all.

11 taxis
+ 12 taxis
23 taxis

Exploring the City

The next day we took a tour on a double-decker bus. We could hop off at the stops. Then we could walk around.

We got off the bus to ride a **trolley**.
A trolley is like a bus on rails.

LET'S EXPLORE MATH

The city bus tour takes 30 minutes. The family also got off to do the 3 other things on the chart below. How many minutes did their whole tour take?

city bus tour	30 minutes
trolley roundtrip ride	20 minutes
hot dog break	15 minutes
picture-taking stop	10 minutes

We ate lunch at the **pier**. We used addition to count the boats that went by.

We saw 12 fishing boats. We saw 15 sailboats too. That means that 27 boats went by as we ate lunch.

12 boats
+ 15 boats
27 boats

We took a ferry for our next trip. We went to a small island. We wanted to see the whole island, so we rented bikes.

We rode on 8 miles of trail! We could see the city and the ocean from the top of a hill on the island.

Bikes cost $12 each hour to rent. Look at this chart. Then answer the questions.

	Cost for 1 hour	Cost for 2 hours	Cost for 3 hours	Cost for 4 hours
Mom's bike	$12	$24	$36	$48
Dad's bike	$12	$24	$36	$48
Maria's bike	$12	$24	$36	$48
Robert's bike	$12	$24	$36	$48
Miguel's bike	$12	$24	$36	$48
Total Cost	?	?	?	?

a. How much does it cost for 1 hour for all of them?

b. How much does it cost for 3 hours for all of them?

c. They rented their bikes at 1:00. They returned the bikes by 3:00. How long did they ride their bikes?

d. How much did they pay to rent the bikes?

15

The City Park

We took the ferry back to the city.
Near the dock was a big park.

We fed the pigeons there. Lots of pigeons came when I threw pieces of my leftover sandwich!

LET'S EXPLORE MATH

There were 15 pigeons on the ground. When Miguel started feeding the pigeons, 19 more pigeons came for food. How many pigeons were on the ground then?

Pigeons were not the only animals at the park. I saw a horse too. A man drove the horse and carriage.

We went for a carriage ride around the park. We waited in line for 15 minutes. The ride took 20 minutes. I added that up. It was 35 minutes altogether.

$$\begin{array}{r} 15 \text{ minutes} \\ + 20 \text{ minutes} \\ \hline 35 \text{ minutes} \end{array}$$

Last Tours

We got to go sailing next. Robert and I got to help raise the sails. A cruise ship was coming into **port**. A cruise ship is a big floating hotel!

Maria counted 32 people on the top deck of the cruise ship. Robert counted 19 people on the middle deck. I counted 26 people on the bottom deck. We saw 77 people in all!

```
  32 people
  19 people
+ 26 people
―――――――――――
  77 people
```

Our next tour was the best of all. We took a helicopter ride! We wore headsets so we could hear the pilot talk.

We saw all the types of transportation that we had traveled in. Everything looked so small!

We used our own transportation on our last day. Our legs! We walked around and bought souvenirs.

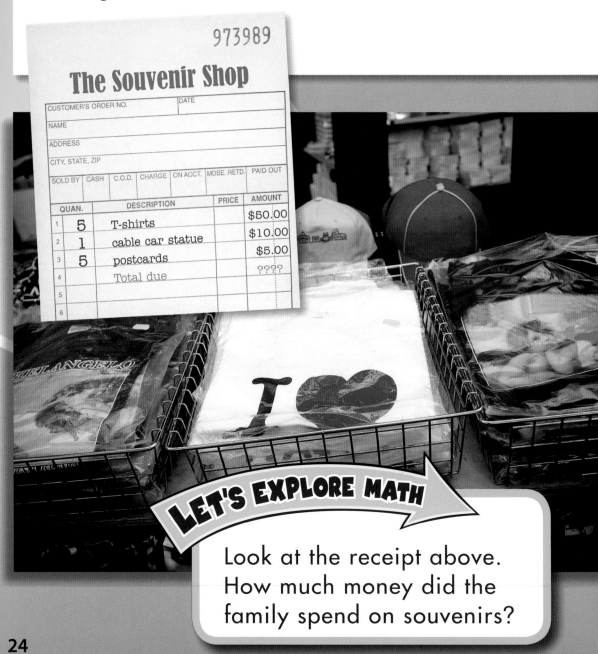

973989

The Souvenir Shop

| CUSTOMER'S ORDER NO. | | | | DATE | | | |

| NAME | | | | | | | |

| ADDRESS | | | | | | | |

| CITY, STATE, ZIP | | | | | | | |

SOLD BY	CASH	C.O.D.	CHARGE	ON ACCT.	MDSE. RETD.	PAID OUT

QUAN.		DESCRIPTION	PRICE	AMOUNT
1	5	T-shirts		$50.00
2	1	cable car statue		$10.00
3	5	postcards		$5.00
4		Total due		????
5				
6				

LET'S EXPLORE MATH

Look at the receipt above. How much money did the family spend on souvenirs?

I worked on my homework the rest of the day. I wrote about all the ways I used addition on this trip. Then we had to pack our bags. We had a late flight home.

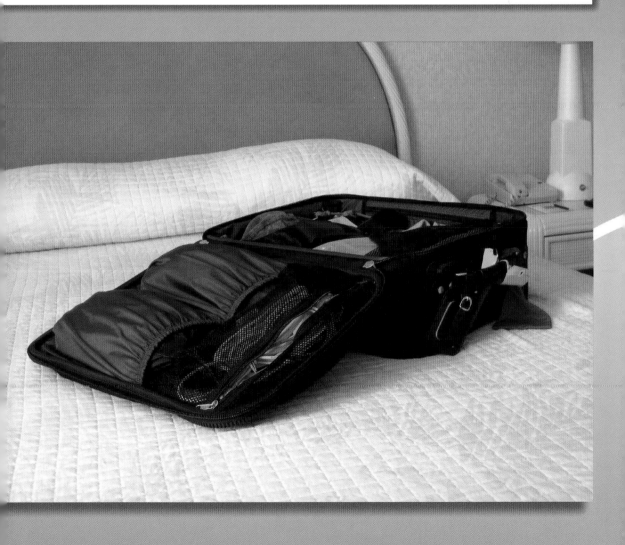

When we left the hotel it was dark outside. But we had one last surprise. There was a limo waiting for us!

Soon we were on the plane. I slept all the way home. Guess what I dreamed about? I dreamed about subways, planes, and ships.

LET'S EXPLORE MATH

Some planes have 3 **cabins**. This chart shows the number of seats in each of the cabins. Look at the chart. Then answer the questions.

Cabin	Number of Seats
first class	12
business class	14
main	70

a. How many seats were in the first class and business class cabins altogether?

b. How many seats were in all 3 cabins together?

c. The pilots have 2 seats. How many total seats are on the whole plane?

Transportation Collections

Marco, Juan, and Chris are friends. The boys like to collect different types of transportation vehicles. They each have a collection of model cars, model trains, and model airplanes. This Saturday they decide to meet at Juan's house to play and trade vehicles. Use the chart below to answer the questions.

Name	Model Cars	Model Trains	Model Airplanes
Marco	45	11	20
Juan	21	10	32
Chris	33	14	13

Solve It!

a. How many model cars do they have in all?

b. How many model trains do they have in all?

c. How many model airplanes do they have in all?

d. Which type of vehicle is their favorite? How do you know?

e. Which type of vehicle is their least favorite? How do you know?

Use the steps below to help you solve the problems.

Step 1: Add together the number of model cars each boy has.

Step 2: Add together the number of model trains each boy has.

Step 3: Add together the number of model airplanes each boy has.

Step 4: Look at the totals to see which type of vehicle has the highest total.

Step 5: Look at the totals to see which type of vehicle has the lowest total.

Glossary

addition—the process of joining 2 or more numbers together to make 1 number called the sum

cabins—the areas inside an airplane where people sit

escalator—a moving stairway

pier—a dock or area where boats are tied up

port—a place where ships can load and unload

transportation—a way to move people and things

trolley—a type of bus that uses rails and electricity to move

Index

Let's Explore Math

Page 6:
a. $20
b. $12
c. $32

Page 11:
75 minutes

Page 15:
a. $60
b. $180
c. 2 hours
d. $120

Page 17:
34 pigeons

Page 24:
$65

Page 27:
a. 26 seats
b. 96 seats
c. 98 seats

Pages 28–29:

Problem-Solving Activity

a. 99 model cars
b. 35 model trains
c. 65 model airplanes
d. model cars; answers will vary.
e. model trains; answers will vary.